EATING YOUR CAKE ...

AND HAVING IT

EATING YOUR CAKE .... AND HAVING IT
Edited by Ann Gray
First Edition 1997
© 1997
All rights reserved
ISBN 0 9525 1551 2

Cover painting 'Custard Darling?'
©Margot Allen

Printed by Pressgang

Published by
Fatchance Press
Elm Court
East St
Sheepwash
Beaworthy
Devon EX21 5NL

Acknowledgements

The Watermelon Sellers (Chris Banks) *Fatchance* Magazine
The Figs And Biscuits I Was Keeping (David Bateman)*From Jellybeans To Reprobation (*Hybrid)
Cooking with Mae West (Judi Benson)   *What   Poets   Eat* (Foolscap), *In The Pockets of Strangers*(Rockingham Press), Turret Books, *International   Wine and Food Society Journal* and BBC Radio
Unrequited (Gillie Bolton) *Seam* Magazine
Aubergine (Patricia Bishop) Headland Press
Perfect Picnic (Anne Born)*Ambit*
Nectarines (Tony Charles) *Acumen*
By The Wayside (Debjani Chatterjee) is reprinted from her first full poetry collection, *I Was That Woman* published by the Hippopotamus Press in 1989
Remembrance (Sarah Cowie) was first broadcast on Merseyside local radio
Oppenheims Cup and Saucer & A Healthy Meal (Carol Ann Duffy) *Standing Femal Nude*, Sleeping *Mean Time*
The Greengrocer makes Love (Alison Dunne) *New Lines from Leicestershire*
our coffee gone cold in its cups (Hilaire) *Fatchance 6*
A Small Hotel (Selima Hill) *A Little Book of Meat* Bloodaxe, How to Be Happy & The Villa *Aeroplanes of the World/Trembling Hearts* Bloodaxe
New Orleans (Linda Lamus) *Quartos Magazine*
Summer Fruits (Margaret Padwick) *Writers Bureau* and *Libra*
Chocolate, With a Glass of Water (William Park) *Ambit* Magazine/Scratch Press
Plum (Mario Petrucci) Shortlisted for 1995 Frogmore Prize
The Secret Life of Aubergines (D Schiller) *Writers News*
Root Vegetable Stew & Mango (M Schneider) *Exits* Enitharmon Press 1994

In Praise of Vodka (Ken Smith) *Tender to the Queen of Spain* (Bloodaxe)

real men don't eat food (Gordon Wardman) *Dog* Magazine/ Odyssey Poets

A Sprig of Chillis (G Warren Wilson) *Staple* Magazine/*Preserving Lemons* Staple First Edition 96

Mustard (Anthony Wilson) *Smiths Knoll* & Basil and Chopped Tomatoes *How Far From Here is Home?* Stride

Like the Blowing of Birds Eggs (Neil Rollinson) *A Spillage of Mercury* Cape Poetry

Fish and Steak (Maurice Riordan) *A Word from the Loki* Faber and Faber 1995

CONTENTS

Introduction   Nigel Slater   9

Judi Benson   10

STARTERS

Gregory Warren Wilson   12
Margaret Kirke   14
Neil Rollinson   15

FISH

David Crystal   18
Sally Young   20
Joan Poulson   21
Peter Carpenter   23
Daphne Schiller   24
Maurice Riordan   25

SORBET

John Daniel   28
Jane Spiro   29
Phil Bowen   31

MAIN COURSE

Myra Schneider   33
Maurice Riordan   35
S R Booth   36
Madeleine Heaney   38
Anne Born   39

Helen Kitson   41
Kathleen Jones   43
Gladys Mary Coles   45
Gillie Bolton   46
Carol Ann Duffy   47

VEGETABLES

Catherine Benson   49
Anthony Wilson   50
Doris Hulme   52
Jane Clarkson   53
Alsion Dunne   54
Daphne Schiller   55
Sid Hoddes   56
Patricia Bishop   57
John Latham   58

CHEESE

John Daniel   61
Chris Banks   62
Mandy Coe   66
Jane Spiro   68
Gregory Warren Wilson   69

FRUIT

Mary Taylor   72
Gregory Warren Wilson   73
Mandy Sutter   74
Debjani Chatterjee   75
Chris Banks   77
Mario Petrucci   79

Myra Schneider	81
Duncan Forbes	82
Hazell Hills	83
Margaret Padwick	84
Joan Poulson	86
Rebecca Goss	87
David Bateman	88
Tony Charles	89
Carol Ann Duffy	92
Ruth L Malkin	93

PUDDINGS

Edmund Cusick	96
Selima Hill	97
Fran Shortridge	101
William Park	102

DRINKS

Ken Smith	104
Gillie Bolton	106
William Oxley	107
Linda Lamus	108
Steve Sims	110
Gordon Wardman	111

COFFEE/TEA/EXTRAS

Hilaire	113
Carol Ann Duffy	114
Yvonne M Fee	115
Sarah Cowie	116

Hazel Jones   117
Joan Poulson   118
Anthony Wilson   120
Mary Maher   121
John Harvey   122

INTRODUCTION by NIGEL SLATER

Only a prude could fail to find food erotic. Feeling the fuzz on the skin of a ripe peach, as you bite into its flesh, its sticky juice running down your chin; pulling open a bulging, ripe fig; eating a salty, quivering oyster. Certainly there is eroticism here, but these are obvious to all. All but a prude, that is.

It is less obvious things about what we buy, cook and eat that are perhaps most interesting - finding a pair of cherries joined at the stalk; gently stirring a pan of thick, dark velvety chocolate; peeling ripe lychees and trying to catch their beads of juice before they fall. Little, personal things. Like sniffing a mushroom cap, buttering the skin of a chicken before it goes in the oven to roast, or rummaging through the leaves of a dark green cabbage to find its hidden pointed heart. To ignore the sensuality of eating, and I would also say cooking, is a crime, but to miss it altogether is a sad thing indeed. I often wonder who could possibly eat a partially melting ice cream without it arousing each and every sense. Who could not get pleasure from peeling a vegetable, or cutting a ripe cheese.

Eating a meal, even a single fruit, and missing its erotic side, is an immeasurable loss. Those who treat food as nothing more than fuel and sustenance are missing as much as those who make love simply in order to procreate. Such pleasure lost.

This collection is a celebration of the erotic pleasure of food, from shopping to cooking to eating. It avoids the obvious, the crude and the unnecessary, offering instead an insight into a side of food that is too often ignored, or sadly, simply unseen.

This book is the work of the generous, those who wish to pass on some of the erotic joy of eating to others. I warmly recommend it to you. And, come on, whose mind does not wander just a little as they sit opposite someone eating a plate of asparagus, lifting the tender stalks from plate to lips?

JUDI BENSON

Cooking with Mae West

You can make a meal of me any day, big boy.
I'm ripe and juicy, nectarine sweet
a tangy little kick on the top of the tongue.

I'm smooth as an avocado
slippery as a trout,
soft as mashed potatoes.

Turn me over-easy, baby.
Look into my golden eye
but don't cut me up.

No dicing, no chopping
just squeeze me, knead me
grind your pepper mill all over my flesh.

A complementary blend
a pinch of this, a knob of that.
Now sprinkle me with culinary kisses.

Keep me on a low heat till I blush pink.
Whisper honey, up and down my spine.
Decorate my naked body with parsley.

Now serve me up on the honeysuckle platter
steaming hot, waiting for you to cool me down.
Hungry now? Bon appetit, big boy.

Starters

GREGORY WARREN WILSON

Ripe Melon

I cut you a slice of cantaloupe.
Your teeth gnaw right down
to the bitter green rind.
I give you more.
Systematic as a wasp
you plunge your mouth
into the segment of sweet flesh
and spit out slithery seeds.
I give you more.
A clown-wide glistening grin
is stencilled on your chin.
There is no more.

I take the fruit-knife and pare
the skin from my ribcage.
Neither of us looks away.
When Marsyas was flayed, you were there.
With my left hand I prize apart
two supple ribs; with my right,
dislocate my pomegranate heart
and place it on your plate
among the crescents of rind.

Meticulous with a toothpick,
you extract from delicate membranes,

from the tissue of valves and ventricles
each crystalline, coagulated drip,
pip by pip.

Relieved by paralysis, I
grow slowly numb, slowly dumb,
feeling, where my pulse once thrummed,
a cavity, and seeing in your eyes
the indifference of depravity.

A Tasty Morsel

When you cooked
corn-on-the-cob
and we sat munching
across the table -
I said -
it reminded me
of Tom Jones
I meant the film - of course
the famous food scene
forgetting that you
are too young
to have seen it.
Don't be filthy
you answered
quick-as-a-flash,
then measured the cob
and assured me
that Tom Jones
has nothing on you.

NEIL ROLLINSON

Like the Blowing of Birds Eggs

I crack the shell
over the bedstead and open it
over your stomach. It runs
to your navel and settles there
like the stone of a sharon fruit.

You ask me to gather it up
and pour it over your breast
without breaking the membrane.

It swims in my palm, drools
from the gaps in my fingers, fragrant,
spotted with blood.

It slips down your chest,
moves on your skin like a woman
hurrying in her yellow dress, the long
transparent train dragging behind.

It slides down your belly and into your
pubic hair where you burst
the yolk with a tap of your finger.

It covers your cunt in a shock
of gold. You tell me to eat,
to feel the sticky glair on my tongue.

15

I lick the folds of your sex, the coarse
damp hairs, the slopes of your arse
until you're clean, and tense as a clock spring.

I touch your spot and something inside you
explodes like the blowing of bird's eggs.

Fish

DAVID CRYSTAL

Cider & Pike

My mouth that loves nipples
is the cracked mud bottom of a pond
that hasn't seen water in weeks.
Rare birds nose in arid fissures
a fish skeleton long since picked clean
a memory of water,
juicy lavas, dragonflies,
misty mornings sucking up frog spawn,
cool pine air.

Go make the tea,
your neck smells like an old shirt, she says.
I'm only aware of a leaf on the bedroom floor,
like a TV advert of a moisturised leaf,
making my rusty Doc Marten fit
for any Ode to Autumn.

Across our communal garden
the tabloid cockney, that works a seven
day week fixing cars & lawnmowers
is filing down his son's teeth with a grinder.
A ritual like making coffee or fishing
for the legendary duck-eating pike wearing
a suit made from fine Irish linen.

Just outside Hereford on a balmy Summer's night
we cooked a pike in cider. Careful of the bones

I nearly choked to death on the bayleaf.
It was a close run thing
& that night I drank to Lady Luck
& our love in blossom
& for once, not a whisper of complaint,
about the washing up.

SALLY YOUNG

Langoustine

Remembering. Our
wet, slippery legs
wrapped around
each other.

The female
and her eggs.

Below the steps
to Montmartre, futile
tears spilt.

It was hard
to digest. This waiting
for your
eyes to sparkle.

JOAN POULSON

Alice B. Toklas Cooks Fish

My grandmother insisted that 'once caught
fish should have nothing more to do with water'.

When Picasso came to lunch I simmered
dry white wine with blade mace,
a leaf from Apollo's laurel and herbs:
thyme, tarragon, rosemary, fresh torn;
earth and sun resonating through my body.....

Later I laid a firm striped bass to poach,
removed it from the fire,
left it to cool in the court-bouillon.

My design was inspired - satin coverlet
of yellow mayonnaise: eggs, green oil.
To amuse, with a pastry tube, swirled
an extravagance of red cream,
not tainted with commercial colouring
but from my own paste
- tomatoes lusciously plumped with sun.
And then cunning detail:
sieved hard-boiled eggs, whites, yolks
kept separate and truffles finely sliced.
A final touch - dusting of fines herbes
with .....my own conceit.....basil.
I was proud of my chef d'oeuvre.

'Incroyable!' Picasso exclaimed
as Helene brought it to table
but Gertrude rocked in silent mirth
when, inflexion of eyebrow perfect-pitched
that one murmured that it might rather
have been sculpted in honour of Matisse.

PETER CARPENTER

Gathering Oysters

No violet evening of lines.
Platforms hosed free of smatterings: silty grot
and clingings of work lap criss-crossed iron
and tarred wood into a still-living fret.

Concrete-middled tyres are belted with mussels left
too long to be good. You expect a weighted corpse
as water levelling with a cement projection
burbles air or splutters phlegm.

Transporters chuff in
and out to serve up their harbourings.
A flight of rungs rusts down to a slurping.
Oiled chains argue. How to gather them?

Clues: plural speckles, burnings, cast-offs;
you crack open one purse after another;
find a saltiness fluent under
the slippage of your tongue.

DAPHNE SCHILLER

Italian Cookery Book

'Polpi affogati.
(Drowned octopus).
If you've been snorkelling and
Have caught your own,
This dish is worth the effort.

Turn the head inside out.
Remove the ink sack, being careful
Of the ink. Pluck out the eyes.
Rinse well. Dispose of hard lumps
In tentacles. Wash away sand
On suction pads. Liquidise tomatoes,
Crush garlic, add oil. Fry it
With chilli. Simmer
Till tender, garnish,
Taste.'

Fine English drizzle soaks my herbs.
No snorkelling today.

MAURICE RIORDAN

Fish

Okay, not the defrosted Sole Florentine
you served the first time you had me around,
nor the oysters, drained from a jar and tossed
with linguine, I rustled up in return.
But what of the scallops bought fresh in Cork,
cautiously nicked of their coral and splashed
with Sancerre, when we had money.
What of our weekly raids on the fish stalls
of Barcelona, for *merluza* (whatever it was),
our ventures with squid, with quenelles
of pike, with pomfret, red mullet, lophius.
And that night on the way from Tarragona
when, our gums watering for the turmeric
and garlic, we bolted a roadside paella.
The light changed to lemon across the bay,
remember, and we stumbled home (home! A
hammock-shaped bed eight stone flights up
in the *barrio gotico*) singing rounds ...

So, we slackened off. But still for birthdays,
for anniversaries, or on a whim, I'd bring home
something from Soper's or from Brewer Street,
and get to work while the babies slept.
If they slept. Scaling, filleting, boning,
absorbed in the smells: fresh, cooked, stale.
We might get somewhere again, I thought, with luck
and persistence. Think of the silky salmon mousse,

the peppery clout of my *bisque Normandie*!
Latterly my tastes veered oriental: saffron,
lemon grass, the cool transparencies of Japan ...
But now what can I do: when, after ten years,
you announce that, truly, you detest fish.

Sorbet

JOHN DANIEL

Rommel's Ice-cream

I called you Rommel because
you were fair with blue eyes
your head rising out of a tank

directing operations
you gave me your recipe
for making lemon ice cream:

Take 3 lemons,
6 ounces of caster sugar
three-quarters of a pint

of double cream
3 tablespoons of iced water.
Grate the rind

Squeeze the juice
Combine with sugar
Whip the cream with iced water

into soft peaks,
Beat in the sweetened lemon juice
and devour

before the tanktracks
churn up the sand
glamourous enemy

JANE SPIRO

Eating Me

tutti frutti
he loves me
vanilla
he loves me not

fat free
he loves me
full-fat cream
he loves me not

colouring preservatives
he loves me
organic sugar-free
he loves me not

freezer packed
he loves me
loose and yielding
he loves me not
　　　*
lingering tongues
I love him
stainless steel spoons
I love him not

slow and langurous
I love him

fast and hot
I love him not

PHIL BOWEN

Orange Maid

liquid roundish bench tree
cool grass stick heat
waves sun wood sea
stem brightly stalk quay

palette savour ice juice
tongue flavour guzzle fruit
drink teeth fresh chew
bite saliva swallow ooze

stain licking squeeze tuck
dissolve want melt love
tingle dripping mine luck
enjoy skin tender suck

pence paper end lid
cold tip spent fridge
finish draining queue sin
out trip till bin

Main Course

MYRA SCHNEIDER

Root Vegetable Stew

When dark nights eat up afternoons
I sweat onions in sunflower oil,
weigh out carrots, a swede,
and tapering baby parsnips
with old-age skins on flesh
that fattened underneath the light
in a cradling of clay, grit, stones.

I take the swede, a misshapen globe
marred with scars, cut it in two.
The apricot bulk makes my head
hum with summer. I slice up
the snow-white parsnips, then tip
lentils, seeds of a butterfly-
petalled plant, into the pan.

Opening the door to throw peelings
in a pail, I bump into snouting cold.
It smells of woodsmoke, bites
as I stare at the park bristled
with black. Frost is stiffening leaves,
grasses, and I feel myself woven
to this land's Saxon past when winter

was a giant who trampled crops in fields,
snuffed breath with icicle fingers -
though this was not the country

of my forbears, though rootlessness
was a wound I bore till turned thirty,
I was warmed enough by love
to put down roots in myself.

When chill sinks its teeth in my ribs,
I retreat to the stove, dip a spoon.
The heat-swollen lentils are melting
among the hulking vegetables,
and yellowbrown as November woods.
I add lemon and fried spices,
stir them in, ladle the stew.

MAURICE RIORDAN

Steak

Just when she thought all that was finished,
it hits her again out of the blue,
slips from her tongue like a swear-word: steak.
And she's gone, not to some wiseacre butcher
who'll fob her off with smiles and a T-bone.
To the supermarkets, where she's free to pinch
and poke, to sniff if need be. And she finds it
at Waitrose (as it happens): a half-pounder,
beautifully marbled and plum-coloured,
reduced to half-price. How that makes her laugh!

(This isn't some 90s anchorite, but one who knows
the business of old: Augustine on his day off.)

Now she is home and, good, they are still out.
She opens the backdoor, windows, the wine.
She reddens the pan, takes the meat to warm
between her palms, then slaps it on ...
Two minutes a side: but hot, hot, hot.
She waives the mushrooms and the onions, just
a tittle of garlic, seasonings, claret.
Does she tremble somewhat? Never mind,
no fat or gristle to speak of. She sits
in the afterglow, dandles her wine, burps.

S R BOOTH

Vindaloo

My love, tonight I offer you India.
My kitchen is dim and cold.
Rain cries at the window and the x-ray buzz
of the fridge
hogs the cool dark.
I heat oil on a high flame
fling in mustard seeds and cardamon pods
reach a hot, smoking, pan-spluttering fragrance.
Smell. Mmm-m.
Yes. Yess.
Do not be embarrassed by your saliva. Swim in it. Drown in it.

Take my silver platter.
Crunch poppadoms. Spicy, crisp. Chew the hot, scented bread.
Slip the silky, spiked Riata gently down your throat.

Once, below a picture of
a spicy, padded tiger
amongst the jangle of sitars
- you fed me Riata.

Try the sweet, sticky, chunky chutneys.
Here.
Take it. Taste it.

Now, I unwrap the garlic from it's white parchment.
The crushed cloves clutch my throat, hands, hair, breath.

I cook the meat, crust and meld it into crumbling,
honey-golden tenderness.
Relax.
Smell the crushed spices of Western India.
Get them into your head
rich and strong.

Exotic, seductive, such aromas. I know it is right.
Soon you will smile and know me.

MADELEINE HEANEY

The Cinderella Hour

The last bus gone,
we huddle in a doorway
eating chips.

You hold me close and
ease one gently through my lips.
I lick the salt from frozen fingers,
suck your thumb.

We curse the cold,
the clock,
our parents
waiting.

ANNE BORN

For A Perfect Picnic

take quails' eggs, firm-boiled,
with iceberg hearts
and velvet mayonnaise.

A smoke salmon pâté
well-pounded by pestle and mortar,
tasty with lemon juice and tomato purée

snug between grainy wholemeal.
Tender chicken breasts
dressed in diaphanous cucumber slices

just faintly salted.
Some almond cakes
whose toasted nuts

crackle like a matchlit fire.
A slim and elegant
vinho verde

and svelte crimson apples
for a last temptation.
Take a moss-green rug

and pick a leafy ceiling
allowing stained-glass sunlight
to blink through.

Sit where the stream
murmurs
the right nothings.

HELEN KITSON

An Anniversary

I try to get it just so:
the setting, a bluebell wood.
A hamper packed
with odourless food.
Things that are easy to digest.
A selection of citrus fruit:
I hold the flesh up to the light,
it's translucent & veined,
like a butterfly's wing.
These details are important:
I could ruin everything
with an egg or an onion.
He's a fussy eater, he insists
on removing every bit of pith
before he'll put an orange
segment in his mouth.
I'm less finicky, I get
pleasure from tearing the
fruit apart, making it mine.
I hand him a brie & grape
baguette but he won't believe
that the grapes are seedless.
He takes them out, squashes
each in turn between thumb
& forefinger. There are no
pips. The fruit has lost
its beauty, it's green mush.

Where we've been sitting
we've spoilt some bluebells,
bruised them
a deeper shade of blue.

KATHLEEN JONES

Witchcraft

Evening.
The lawn is dark as blood
beyond the window's slanted shaft.
I close the curtains on its secret shade
to practise ancient skills.

I polish wood, smooth linen,
sharpen the knives,
prepare a table for the sacrament of meat
place silver, flowers, candles.
A nightly ceremony.

Bright as a sword my mirror-image
sheathes herself in red.
My skin is smooth - young almost -
but my hands are strong and cruel.

Tonight six guests
await a miracle.

Annointing their plates
with some strange mixture
conjured of chocolate, orange rind and rum,
swirling their conversation round me like a robe,
my charm - fatal as hemlock -
binds them within the circle
of my skill.

The moon's egg-yellow, empty plate
determines time.
Soon, someone's head will be upon my pillow
and I will drink his blood
before the sun's first ray
touches the key-stone.

GLADYS MARY COLES

To Make A Morsel Tender

First catch your person
examine for decay.
Remove all outer wrappings.
Rub. Powder. Pat.
Turn over - same again.
Pull off all metal rings
(especially those given by another).
Place on a clean sheet.
Turn up the temperature.

GILLIE BOLTON

Guide to Healthy Living, an extract

six thick slices of wholemeal bread
every day will give essential trace
elements and offer bowel regularity
for mental balance with vitality of
nerves you require physical contact
get yourself a cat or give a little
more time to the stages of foreplay
avoidance of stimulating substances
gives a sense of constant normality
water to drink will cleanse kidneys
eat no chocolate or cream they will
clog arteries and create blackheads
ball-games sex and jogging exercise
and strengthen a variety of muscles
always go to sleep early and get up
as soon as you waken be careful not
to lie-in eight hours complete rest
are essential try the new positions
as illustrated below for recreation

CAROL ANN DUFFY

A Healthy Meal

A Gourmet tastes the secret dreams of cows
tossed lightly in garlic. Behind the green door, swish
of oxtails languish on an earthen dish. Here are
wishbones and pinkies; fingerbowls will absolve guilt.

Capped teeth chatter to a kidney or at the breast
of something which once flew. These hearts knew
no love and on their beds of saffron rice they lie
beyond reproach. What is the claret like? Blood.

On table six, the language of tongues is braised
in armagnac. The woman chewing suckling pig
must sleep with her husband later. Leg,
saddle and breast bleat against pure white cloth.

After *calf* to *veal* in four attempts. This is
the power of words; knife, tripe, lights, charcuterie.
A fat man orders his *rare* and a fine sweat
bastes his face. There are napkins to wipe the evidence

and sauces to gag the groans of abattoirs. The menu
lists the recent dead in French, from which they order
offal, poultry, fish. Meat flops in the jowls. Belch.
Death moves in the bowels. You are what you eat.

Vegetables

CATHERINE BENSON

Garlic

I choose the plumpest head from the pottery bowl,
the bowl we bought in France eight years ago.
The cloves blush purple through tissue paper skin,
rounded bottoms in tight, white trousers.
I choose the plumpest clove, prise it free.
The skin whispers between my stripping fingers,
a few white flakes fall to the floor.
My thumb-nail pierces the flesh,
and summer meals, al fresco, ooze from my memory;
olive-oil dressing, salad, sun and sea.

Crisp lettuce, sweet tomatoes, tart lemons, soft bread
are spread on a table set with lantern and wild flowers,
you, barbecuing sardines.
Afterwards we walked along the beach
hoarding the day, the summer, our freedom,
parcelling up our store of memories
for this time of garlic-laced winter stews.
I cut and chop, and scrape oily slivers
from sticky fingers and later, in bed, you taste
my fingers. "Mmm - garlic," you say. "Remember ...."

Basil and Chopped Tomatoes

Too many (poems) seemed to be about cutting up basil and tomatoes while Mozart played. Liz Lochhead, Observer, 13/3/94.

There are too many poems
with basil and chopped tomatoes
in them. This will not be
one of them. Nor will Mozart

play in the background, nor soft
breezes delicately waft through
the kitchen. Probably it will
be Desert Island Discs

and chicken casserole while you read
the Sunday papers. We do not
have a cat so the cat will not
appear, hungrily. The baby -

is the baby allowed to be present?
It will be its first week
of sitting up on its own in
the playpen. If not it will be crying.

The poem is almost completed
but one feels it lacks imagery.
Ever dropped a tin of tomatoes
onto a hot pan of garlic

and chillies in extra virgin oil?
You don't need a poet to help you.
If you get the timing just right
it sounds like a round of applause.

DORIS HULME

You're Not My Sunshine

You are my pumpkin
my luscious pumpkin. I tear
your heart out, it's in the way.

Insert my candle and get you
glowing, then eat you
for dinner next day.

JANE CLARKSON

Mushroom

O.K., here's the deal:
you keep me in the dark,
feed me any old shit -
I don't care.
When I'm full fruited,
and you're in the mood,
eat me,
with garlic and butter
- or anything you fancy -
I'm easy.

ALISON DUNNE

The Greengrocer Makes Love

Seeing heat sealed cucumbers
earth under his fingernails

weighs her breasts in his hands
dreams of perfect apples

spins her through his fingers
twists and seals himself inside

muttering of past their best
ranunculus, half price.

She remembers the pork butcher
in an alley between the shops
wrapping her in
fresh white paper hands.

Not thinking of meat.

DAPHNE SCHILLER

The Secret Life of the Aubergine

A whale of a vegetable
Rolls in my rack, its
Sleek dark contours
Fatly glowing. It welcomes me
To a purple world where
Bruises blossom on papery skin,
Grapes cascade like velvet eggs,
Hedges open a violet eye.
Here indigo seas sway damson weed
And tumbling deep in the ocean wastes
Aubergines sing with earthquake voice
Blowing their dreams to the sky.

SID HODDES

Mashed Potato

If I ever had to choose between you
and a third helping of mashed potato,
(Whipped lightly with a fork
not whisked,
and a little pool of butter
melting in the middle ...)

I think
I'd choose
the mashed potato.

But I'd choose you next.

PATRICIA BISHOP

Aubergine

Nothing is more beautiful
than this aubergine.
A musk of purple sheen
scented with earth
as it lay pregnant on straw.

Its green calyx still hugs
the great and gorgeous bulge.

I place it
on an orange plate,
on a brown table.
All day I have come
to look, to touch,
to stroke.

Ayatollah Khomeni warned the maidens
this fruit from Eden could tempt
them to immodest thoughts.
How wrong the Ayatollah.

Aubergine is a gravid woman,
a queen, her skin locked satin,
her colour arousal.

JOHN LATHAM

Out Of The Salad Bowl ......

She's tossing us. We wheel and plunge an emerald sky
helter-skelter slick on olive oil
a mushroom waltzes with a cauliflower slice
a thirsty curl of anchovy salt-trails me, dabs me dry.

Blandishments of carrots, corn, a cucumber's soft suck
tomato kiss, embrace of avocado
a spinach leaf cavorts and flops exhausted
runner beans careen around the bowl, riding their luck.

Parsley snags and tickles, fresh garlic makes me high
spices stab me, peppers flick their tails,
sunflower seeds fleck lettuce and alfalfa,
a pallid radish ricochets, crash-lands, scutters by.

I'm forked, suspended, terrified, inches from her face
her breath alive with marjoram and sage,
her teeth - froth-studded - hover, glisten
frame a throbbing half-light, a silent, scarlet place

into which I'm guided, plucked smoothly off the prong,
I wallow in warm juices, sudden dark,
a cavern full of waterfalls, a grating.
Too tipsy to resist the massive suction of her tongue

I'm swirled, half-drowning, nibbled, licked and teased,
she slides along the length of me,

her pauses make me wild. Before
she gulps me down, she's done exactly as she pleased.

JOHN DANIEL

Heavenly Cheeses

Puritan cheeses
cut with a wire
upright as Sunday School

square canaries on doorsteps
perched on crackers,
pecking the cheeks of aunts -

It wasn't until I met
Brie in round boxes
 Les Anges d'Or,

and Camembert,
 wrapped in vestments,
from Normandy

smelling of cowsheds
and melting women,
I ascended to heaven.

CHRIS BANKS

My Darling Cheese

1
I want to know.
Do you break or melt
or crumble? Do you bite
electric on the palate?
Are you salt, smooth, creamy,
slightly sweet?
Oh let me lick and nip
and nibble, sink my teeth,
my tongue, deep into
your slab, your wedge,
your chunks, your curves,
your crevices.
I want to taste you, cheese.

2
Have you ever had
an intimate relationship
with cheese? It's disgusting.
Especially blue veined cheese.
Think of it: sour milk churned up.
Imagine putting that into your mouth.
Cheese is seething with disease.
I warn you, stay away from it.

3
I have committed to this cheese
because I want to share
its yellow loneliness,
its salt existence. I want
to truly know this cheese.
I have opened
to the influence
this cheese brings to my life.
I am learning from its strength,
its stoical endurance.
Also, I have seen beyond
its tough exterior
to what is soft
and fragile in this cheese -
though we are talking here survivor.
When I take this cheese inside me,
I can trust
that I have all I need.
I give my gratitude to God
for bringing
this ripe cheese
into my world.

4
It's bloody typical of cheese
to run away
as soon as things hot up.
Take it from me,
I know cheese backwards.

Listen love, there are just two sorts,

at least in England.
One's mild and pale and bland,
the consistency of wet
elastic bands without the pull;
the other strong, mature -
at any rate in terms of cheese.
And tasty. You end up wanting more.
But don't expect this cheese
to hang around.

Cheese! You know,
there isn't one
whose whole life-purpose
isn't just to lie
between two bits of bread
or spread across a biscuit.

5
Dear Leicester.
For some time now, I have felt in need
of something more than you can give.
Call it subtlety perhaps, sophistication.
As you know, my situation's changed
since first I picked you off the shelf
at Tesco's. This house, for instance.
My career, travel, the European influence.

You may have heard me mention Roquefort.
Forgive me, Leicester, I confess
I have become acquainted rather well
with Roquefort on my weekend trips to France.
I do not mean to twist the knife,

but Roquefort's so distinctive, so insistent.
Though I have exercised restraint,
I fear that after last week's fondue party
I can no longer help myself.
I'm sorry, Leicester; we must go
our separate ways. Please don't weep too much.
It doesn't suit your constitution.

For ever,
Your Ryvita.

MANDY COE

Go To Bed With A Cheese & Pickle Sandwich

Go to bed with a cheese and pickle sandwich
- it is life enhancing.
It doesn't chat you up
- *you* have to make *it*.

A cheese and pickle sandwich
is never disappointing.
You don't lie there thinking:
Am I too fat?
Too insecure?
Too fertile?

Your thoughts are clear
- your choices simple:
to cut it in half,
or not to cut it in half.
How thin to slice the cheese,
and where you should place the pickle.

From a cheese and pickle sandwich
you do not expect flowers,
poems, words of love and acts of adoration.
You expect what you get
- cheese .... and pickle.

You want, you eat,
and afterwards - you have eaten.

No lying awake resentful
listening to it snore.

Safe snacks.
It comes
recommended.

JANE SPIRO

making cheese

start with the juices

filter through fishnet
till drops are turned
to liquid silk

place in mould
of brown hands tanned
in caresses

throw to dry
on a hot floor baked
in several slow summers

peel away rind
when flesh is lightly peached
like a baby's cheek

serve warm and white
with white wine
silk and deep pillows

GREGORY WARREN WILSON

A Sprig of Chillies

I send you poems like pale cheeses;
carefully moulded,
a whiff of sheepishness about them -
experience curdled and preserved
in tidy rinds, endstopped lines.

They travel well,
these demure English cheeses;
never cause a stink
of putrefaction, or blocked sinks.

The sprig of chillies you sent me
smoulders.
Seedpods pointy as stiletto heels
and patent-leather shiny
turn the kitchen into a red light district.
Shall I make *spaghetti alla putanesca*?

You lay out your needs on Tuscan sheets -
perishable soft-fruit on table linen.
Thumbing your letter, I thumb you
as if selecting the sweetest nectarine,
the juiciest melon, feeling for bruises -
deliberate, intent.

We've agreed on terms;
bartering packets of Earl Grey tea

and carefully turned phrases
for your temperament,
your unpredictable phases,
your glass jars of jam and jelly
distilled from fruits in an orchard where,
towards sunset on summer evenings,
famished mosquitoes whinge,
and at night a porcupine claws the gate's hinge.

Putana: Italian slang for prostitute.
Spaghetti alla Putanesca: a hot Neapolitan dish

Fruit

MARY TAYLOR

Pomegranate

Nipples hard as stars
cusps sharp around
a sticky dust of anthers.

Tonight, I will let you
gently tear my chiffon veil

reveal the chambers of my heart.
A honeycomb of ivory seed
a casket of ruby crystals.

You will prise them out
one by one
amber, rosé, crimson

bittersweet moments on your tongue
gone before you can savour
memory and myth

with each seed
you will almost taste me
yet your thirst is never quenched
for still you do not know me.

GREGORY WARREN WILSON

Know The Feeling?

Now you're going halfway round the world;
what can I give you
that's light and flatpacks
into an envelope?

No more love poems;
tricksy images and all that.
No: something bitter
sweet.

Here's the peel from a navel orange
all in one piece:
the bit that's left
when the flesh has gone.

Mercator's projection?
No. One strip
thumb-scooped from pole to pole,
and two half-globes.

Press its creamy pith
to your belly,
navel to navel,
skin to skin,

and think of me.

MANDY SUTTER

Figs

He brings me figs; whole dried figs from Izmir.
They don't look much; a bagful of coagulated crusts
and twisted stalks, the life pressed out of them;
roudels of dun rubber; bellies of old, spent men.

He takes one out and touches it, clammy to my lips.
I make a face and won't open, but he holds it there
till its burnt treacle scent widens my nostrils; has me
biting hard into the fig's hide. It's like biting card;

bits in my mouth; I could spit. But taste works in,
stronger than a plum, sparer than toffee. Grainy
seeds, like negligible bones, give the pleasure bite
and sticky fur leaves its trace on his fingers.

DEBJANI CHATTERJEE

By The Wayside

It should not be broken against the skull;
it should bring a smile to your face, not tears.

Buy one for its verdant beauty, its firm smooth skin,
curve your hands around the voluptuous oval,
breathe in its tangy vibrant scent of woodland grove,
lift it in your palm, feel the luscious weight:
bigger is better, heavier more heavenly.
Shake it about and the swirling pool will whisper
promises, once released.

Then bargain with the vendor who already knows
that you must have it. Wait by the wayside for him
to strike at its crown in slicing petal patterns
and to decapitate it with a single blow
of his blade, and so present you, with a flourish,
liquid delectation.

It is the milk of natural kindness.
Drink in the tropics, waving seas, palm trees,
and stillness sliding down your sun-drenched throat
till the last caressing drop is possessed.

Then watch the knife descend in cleaving strokes
dissecting inner walls and so reveal
the white flesh inviting, ripe for biting.

Dig deeply and scrape it from the shell, and savour
the succulent serendipity, the flavour
of earthy fantasy. Its flesh is sensuous:
a chewy cool delight.

A feast for sight and palate: meal complete,
a coconut is nature's milk and meat.

CHRIS BANKS

The Watermelon Sellers

In Spain, her sixteenth summer,
the watermelon sellers
called to her on every street,
coaxed her with the unfamiliar fruit,
sliced it, beckoned her to taste.

From whole green footballs
issued smiling crescents,
luscious, red as inner lips,
that oozed their juices
when she bit skin deep.

She slurped the liquid,
spat away the flat black pips.
A rivulet of juice
snaked down her arm.
Her parched throat opened.

So fresh the watermelon tasted
while the sun was turning her to gold.
As the sea sluiced over her
so sweet the flesh. The world,
the world was ripening.

She took it in her hands and ate.
And her breasts were new moons
under her bikini
and the sand hot silk
beneath her toes.

MARIO PETRUCCI

Grapes

How carefully you plied me, pouting
as you popped them in - till I sussed

you'd giggle and your eyes shine
if I sucked them, pouted them back, the skin

polished with my spit, too slippery
for you to retrieve, and me too quick,

so we'd be left there, with your thumb
in the *moue* of my lips, so I bit

but only half-strength, to heave you
overbrimming, into another sister's kiss

half-cocked on my mouth.

MARIO PETRUCCI

Plum

Love,
take this plum, here
from my palm, take it quickly
between your teeth; let your tongue
try   its blue bloom of chalk, roll across
its taut silk; briefly, brush the tight zero
of the absent stalk; plumb the cleft. The bite -
feel indigo split, slide like lava-skin over yellow
sweetness, tart metal, the fine textures of flesh
slithering numb past enamel, butting against the
bulge of gums, until - at last - you meet the
stone - its dense unyielding, its size,
the ridge of bone-wood round its rim
holding, within, everything
you've been led to.

MYRA SCHNEIDER

The Mango

lies cool in the palm of my hand,
egg of a mythical bird. It's reddened
like a path over the Caribbean Sea
I tried to catch in the camera's box.
Cutting into this fruit tonight

I'm slicing the sun. Its gorgeous flesh
is yellow and boned by a stone flat
as an oar. I hold up a sliver - it shines
in the darkening blue of the windowpane.
Juice drips from elbow and chin.

'You must eat a mango in the bath,'
said the old lady shut in a dim
upstairs flat in a cathedral city
in England, after a lifetime
of Trinidad's sprawling heat.

The pulp is more generous than peach,
rich as laughter, carries a trace
of jasmin, melts my mouth. I'm feeding
body and mind on mellowed sun.
If this were religion I'd believe it!

DUNCAN FORBES

A Better Berry

"Doubtless God could have made a better berry, but
doubtless God never did." Dr Boteler quoted by Izaak Walton

Reach down between the green serrated groves
And feel for berries' ripened crimson selves
Wearing their seeds like buttons on a sofa,

Twiddle the six-point star of Bethlehem
Between your pink forefinger and your thumb
To reinvent the wheel with leaf and stem,

Then with some Amaretto - just a splash -
Taste at its best, sun-ripened and picked fresh,
The veiny brainwork of the sweetened flesh

With caster sugar crystals by the spoonful
And cream poured in a languid waterfall
Onto the waiting strawberries in bowl,

Then savour both the shape in the saliva
And that infallible midsummer flavour
As if you were in love and it your lover,

Moving the proof from lips to uvula
And swallow, swallow till the fever's over,
As if in heaven and an unbeliever.

HAZELL HILLS

A Fruitful Spell

Stimulate your hidden passions.
Make your partial life complete.
Turn three times.
Repeat these rhymes:

"What I am is what I eat -
Ruby Mango, Star Fruit, Citron.
Rambutan and Cardamom.
Pomegranate. Tamarillo.
Medjool Dates, Cinnamon.
Kiwano, Pitahaya.
Granadilla. Ginger Root.
Kumquat, Magosteen, Papaya,
Coconut, Passion Fruit".

Savour each one as you say it.
Suck the essence. Resolute
full fruition
it is your mission.

This charm's power is absolute.

MARGARET PADWICK

Summer Fruits

Together we picked raspberries,
strawberries, currants,
cramming them into punnets
warm and juicy
on the hottest day of summer;
gathering recklessly
more than we could eat,
kissing among the canes
with sticky mouths.
Dripping with juice,
packed into baskets
swung on sunburnt arms,
they trailed us home.

Then, sorcerers
in my small kitchen
we laughed and sweated
among bubbling pans
of jam and jellies,
wrote names on labels
smeared blood-red.

Later you packed the still-warm jars
greedily, more than your due,
into a suitcase

leaving a few for me
cooling on the sill,
to eke out your memory
with winter toast.

JOAN POULSON

In Roman Provinces

they cook quince in wine,
strain the gritty pulp into a pancheon,
trail in honey.

As the liquid thickens
they add ginger, cinnamon and galingale,
gasping at nectarous bronze firmness
burning like the sun
in the back of the throat.

A Portuguese sailor describes it
quince sweetmeat to his wife
in tones so warm and livened
she would make it also -

stirs the molten gold
marmelo ...marmelo ....marmelo

You, Genius

Did your
academic day
involve
sucking the flesh
from
one pear
and feeling the
juice

       s
      l
       i
        d
         e

to your elbow?

I am waiting
for you to put
down
that paper
and watch me
take off this dress.

DAVID BATEMAN

The Figs And Biscuits...

I've just eaten the figs and biscuits I was keeping
      for when you came.
When I realised you weren't coming,
I figured I might as well.

They were all good, but frankly,
there was twice as much as I wanted.

I think I'm going to be lovesick.

TONY CHARLES

Nectarines

Evenings in my room,
I play a mind game:
I imagine you
eating fruit, your firm
teeth breaking the crisp
flesh; your darting tongue.

Nobody else could
eat fruit quite like that,
just as no-one else
could flick back her hair
the way you did, or
kiss me with her eyes.

If the best of all
insecurities
is to travel with
no destination,
so that the movement
becomes its own end,

Then the best of all
lives is when we do
nothing that we've planned.
In such a moment
we met: I recall
dull sunlight, your smile.

But sometimes it's good
to plan things, small things;
make the day a game
of little rhythms,
flashes of laughter
that hold back the dark.

So I've been shopping;
I've bought a punnet
of fresh nectarines.
Each evening this week
I'll eat one, slowly,
thinking about you.

TONY CHARLES

Wimbledon Fortnight

Dressed
in white flickering,
on screen, phlunk of the balls,
soft grunts of effort,
applause

pause
while we play out
our endless deuces -
your advantage,
mine -

wine
in cool glasses
and licking crushed strawberries
from the hollow between your
breasts.

CAROL ANN DUFFY

Sleeping

Under the dark warm waters of sleep
your hands part me.
I am dreaming you anyway.

Your mouth is hot fruit, wet, strange,
night-fruit I taste with my opening mouth;
my eyes closed.

You, you. Your breath flares into fervent words
which explode in my head. Then you ask, push,
for an answer.

And this is how we sleep. You're in now, hard,
demanding; so I dream more fiercely, dream
till it hurts

that this is for real, yes, I feel it.
When you hear me, you hold on tight, frantic,
as if we were drowning.

Bruises

I listen to the traffic, because it means I don't have to listen to my thoughts.I do the housework, even my ironing, even washing the kitchen floor behind the fridge, sweeping away the fuzzy blue raisins, other unidentifiable rotten objects, dirt that has accumulated there. But my energy runs out suddenly, like a car running out of gas, and I stop, drink coffee.

Last night I cooked for you. You arrived, a little late, as you always do. (I time the dinner to compensate, as usual.) You ran your fingers through your hair when I let you in, and apologised, out of habit.

We kissed. I dished up. We ate. The evening wore on. You grew fidgety.

"What's wrong?" I said.

"Nothing," you were quick to say. "Still a bit hungry. Got any fruit or anything?"

There was an apple in the dish. It was a red apple, bruised, going soft with age.

"Half each." I carried it into the kitchen and sliced through the wrinkling peel, carved out the bruises as best I could, sprayed the exposed flesh with lemon juice to prevent it from browning in the air.

I sat on the floor at your feet, my arm entwined around your knees and we bit into our apple; exclaimed at the sharpness of the lemon juice, the sweetness of the milky centre. My hands were sticky. I wiped them on your jeans. You protested. I moved my hand to your inner thighs, your flies, teasing strokes now. Your protests faded as you swelled under my hands, became reluctant grunts of submission. I pulled you down onto me - unbuttoning, unzipping, removing - on the floor by the sofa. We made love, stickily.

And then you wouldn't look me in the eye, just like a man after a one night stand. And told me what you'd come prepared to say. And left me, with the bruises.

Puddings

EDMUND CUSICK

Reading Your Lips

Your timing perfect, you have slipped
to the ladies, leaving me poised
between coffee and dessert, fantasy
and fulfilment. So I touch the spoon,
warm from your hand, that you held,
an inch from your lipstick,
as you spoke, paused, almost embraced
the heaped mound of cream, ice cream,
hot chocolate fudge, then waited,
and spoke again, hesitated,
opened to take it -
and again delayed, teasing it
until I took it from you, guided it
between your parted lips, felt
it press inside, your tongue easing
and releasing a quarter-mouthful
of pleasure. Then, as I withdrew,
the soft, slight tug as your lips
pouted to suck it clean.

I do not know if, after this, we will
go home together. Somehow
it no longer matters.

SELIMA HILL

How To Be Happy

In the crowded hold of someone's boat,
chocolate sauce is being poured on pears
that shudder as the chocolate coats their shoulders
and spreads its lip across each tilted plate,
across the laps of guests, the rubber floor,
till everything is sunk in utter darkness,
and no one speaks, and no one even moves.
Years go by; then someone's eyes make out
the polished surface of a chocolate sea
where tiny golden boats are busy fishing.

SELIMA HILL

A Small Hotel

My nipples tick
like little bombs of blood.

Someone is walking
in the yard outside.

I don't know why
Our Lord was crucified.

*A really good fuck
makes me feel like custard.*

SELIMA HILL

The Villa

His famous cock
that he goes on about's
about as much fun
as a frozen lamb,
and I just ran away
across the heath
one night;
I left the moonlit villa
far behind
the helicopters, chainsaws,
parrots, knives,
and little maids who specialise
(he gives them sweets)
in screaming
at the parrots;
I slipped away,
and came back
here,
to you:
breathing gently
like a giant flower
smelling of custard
being stirred,
and licked -
custard
made of eggs
and warm vanilla pods

where egg-white islands
shunt
their sugar bays.

FRAN SHORTRIDGE

Dessert

take two bananas
slice and
lay side by side

sprinkle with
dark brown sugar
and a generous
amount of rum

bake for
twenty minutes
until tender

serve with
whipped cream

perfect
when the mood
is for something
exotic
tempting

wickedly
delicious

or
you could
just call me

WILLIAM PARK

Chocolate, With A Glass Of Water

Tore the wrapper off: ate chocolate.

From the cow: fat man with udders,
who spurted milk, creamy

dairy fresh, where it huddled
in a crate. To the winding road,

milkman on doorstep,
pouch of gold, Christmas tip.

I had chocolate: broke it crazy.
Brown plastic, I slid on sweetly.

Water out of the tap: policeman
liquefied beneath his steel helmet.

The chocolate soft in my throat, sexy.
The water chasing it, chasing it.

Drinks

KEN SMITH

In Praise of Vodka

The taste they say for they must
or they feel that they must so they say
so they say they say *it has none,*
there's no taste, just water.

Water: the glassy lake Christ trod,
a bowl Herod rinsed his fingers in,
the rain falling on Troy's ruins,
last word last balm of the living.

The same water, over and over. They say
for they say for they must so they say
we're running out running dry but there's always
the same amount as there's always been.

It's we who are more. As for myself
I've spent all my days working out
just what little Miss Peaches might like
and I'm due a day off for the rest of my life.

So out of the freezer the bottle, the green
frosty bottle, its label iced in cyrillic,
the glass and the water beside the glass.
Russische. Moskovskaya. Stolichnaya.

So this is the taste of nothing:
nothing then nothing again. Nothing at all.

The taste of the air, of wind on the field,
the wind through the long wet forest.

A stream and the rain. I lie in my yard
and open my mouth to the moon and the down falling rain
and the rods of its words speak over my tongue
to the back of my throat and they say

Voda
Water
Vodka

Voda
Water
Vodka

Voda
Water
Vodka

Voda
Water
Vodka

Voda
Water
Vodka

GILLIE BOLTON

Unrequited, unspoken

My blood races to catch you -
dammed, it chokes me.

I raise my glass, but
wine
pours down my chest;

with you so near I lose
where my mouth is,
where I end and you begin.

WILLIAM OXLEY

Sweet. Heart

The long avenues of imagined happiness
Bacchus brings.
Crazy twisted vines, jungle things,
and grapes bunches of green brains
or addled purple cells,
seen in Carinthia once or France
and elsewhere.

Like stretched bell-notes glugging out
and each cellar-smelling bottle labelled like
postage-stamp Cezanne or pseudo-
Van Gogh. South tasting wine

its bouquet of Loire or Provence
knocked off clouds by swallows' wings
or wind-sucked scents of thyme and briony.

Then in tall glasses the flush of love,
liquid roses, on a million tables making
old, old words new again. Sweet.   Heart.

LINDA LAMUS

New Orleans

I sit by the Mississippi,
cottonball moon rising twice
over sluggish brown water.

Adulterating a double
shot of honey vodka with ice,
coldness shocks my fingers,
freezes my lips to an 'O' bubble.
A breeze drifts across my skin, eases
away a sultry July day.
Cool liquid lingers on my tongue,
surfs down my throat in a thick wave,
spinning half-remembered senses
into overstrung.

My third double slug. A tattered
black musician with half an ear
limps along the riverbank, sax
sleazing love songs, thrilling
anybody near.

Menace hangs
heavy as jasmine
on thick air beyond the endless
mardi gras of the French Quarter.
And the violence of Storyville
where unwary souls are ghettoed and knifed,

joining the dead in St. Louis Cemetery
for a ten dollar spike.

Fifth double shot and I don't care;
everything washes over me.
Marie Laveau, Voodoo Queen,
is strutting her stuff, weaving her spell -
a special love gris gris.
A jumbalaya of oysters
slipping, honey sliding, juices
oozing from secret bayous,
jazz jumping at Preservation Hall
and two-tone tapdancers hanging loose.

Seventh slouble dug - I fear
a crazy dog ran past, laughing,
chewing half an ear ......

STEVE SIMS

Better than it ever was

Best is memory

Clothes horse the floor
make the room look lived

She clears a space
glows from the bath
smiles Kiss my nipples
licks him proud
through rum
that's sugar-rimmed

He is paralysis
needs her kick-start
for a genesis

She joins him to the bed
where they mull
life histories

He sniffs a future
till at last
she drops out
of focus.

GORDON WARDMAN

real men don't eat food

- you seen this menu? Says Tam,
    I mean, what's a *gammon muffin*, for christ's sake?
    It sounds like a sexual perversion

Hank's got his back to the landlord,
pouring a dram from a smuggled bottle
into an empty lager glass
to go with their pints of bitter
-    yeah, once a pub thinks it's a restaurant
    it's halfway to being a knocking shop;
    see a man enjoying his scran
    you can bet there's nookie around

-    it's all gone to hell, right enough,
    since they started serving women

Hank passes him the gill -
they've had this conversation a thousand times
but it's an undemanding vintage

-    I remember when pubs were pubs

-    and a man went home for the other

Coffee/Tea
Extras

HILAIRE

our coffee gone cold in its cups

you bring out from your bag a mandarin
& roll it slowly between your hands to loosen its skin
as you begin to tell me about the friendship which has just ended.
this morning a friend rang you to say she does not want to see you
again
because you are too observant.
you take note of things she tells you,
& make mention of them in later letters or conversations.
she finds this oppressive.
you begin to peel the mandarin
piling the skin carefully in a saucer
& say:*that's another friendship over,*
there's not many left now.
with your fingernails you pick off bits of pith
& scatter the small white threads around you
as you try to make sense of what she has said.
it seems a curious accusation.
you split the fruit & offer me half.
lack of attention would cause me more offence, I say,
& segment by segment
we dissect the remains of this friendship,
chewing over its outcome
& spitting pips into the saucer.
that night, undressing for bed,
I find two strings of pith lodged in my shoes
where they had been brushed distractedly from your lap.
I trust you will forgive me for noticing

Oppenheim's Cup and Saucer

She asked me to luncheon in fur. Far from
the loud laughter of men, our secret life stirred.

I remember her eyes, the slim rope of her spine.
This is your cup, she whispered, and this mine.

We drank the sweet hot liquid and talked dirty.
As she undressed me, her breasts were a mirror

and there were mirrors in the bed. She said Place
your legs around my neck, that's right. Yes.

YVONNE M FEE

Four O'Clock Fantasy

I look at you with lust - so smooth and long,
So firm, cream-filled, yet softening to my tongue,
Your sleek, smooth covering heaven to my eyes.
My conscience pricks. I know I am unwise.

Your sensuous shapeliness invades my soul
With urgent passion to consume you, whole.
In my desire to press you to my lips
I feel you slinking slowly to my hips.

It breaks my heart to leave you lying there ...
'Yes - how much is that chocolate eclair?'

SARAH COWIE

Remembrance

I put you in my mouth
this bread is my body he said
take eat
the experience gripped me
my empty senses haunt me
they were full of the juice of the now
but now, I am impregnated with a shadow
fill me fill me
your body, put to warm
between the sheets
like hot bread nestled in a basket and napkin
crusty and fragrant
steam rises from your flesh
when I break you open
white soft centre
fill me fill me
take eat
with this remember me
how can I forget
the sweet drink
the fang
the serum
purging in me
this is my blood

HAZEL JONES

Narcissa's Last Orchid

Narcissa waits. Her thighs cool
on magenta sheets. Painted shutters
bar the afternoon, mute the traffic
two floors below. Downtown stores
close against the heat. Overhead a fan
beats air. Narcissa strokes her skin.
Oyster silk and crêpe-de-Chine drape
the wicker chair. The oils are ready
in stoppered jars. She stirs vermouth
with a cocktail spoon, slides ice
across her tongue. Black olives
mist an eggshell bloom on porcelain.
The doorway. The orchid
wide in your hand. You go in.

(Narcissa's Last Orchid is the title of a painting by Georgia O'Keefe)

JOAN POULSON

The King Was In -

That meal last night too rich   too much
and later
our bedroom chokingly hot.

She lay beside me
breath light as moths wing
eyelids   indigo-fringed   fluttering on her cheeks
pillow-soft body resistant as flint
her sleep unbroken.

Now she paces the corridors
new robe hissing round her ankles
fingers lingering over stitchery   hips prominence
curve of thigh

caressing silken bees   padded plump
on mulberry taffeta.
I smell her skin   sugared cinnamon
through my locked door
feel its sheen against my palm

curve my thumb around
this guinea's perfection   lay it
lip overlapping lip on this glistening mound ....
But must lie down   rest   my chest iron-bound
by her

entering her parlour
leaving the door open so I hear her
humming her songs
creamy throat vibrating
coiled red-gold braids framing the waxed oval of her face.

Clink of spoon on pot
scooping-up mounds of pollened sweetness
seeking   fragments of comb.

Soon she will replace the lid
return   rattle the handle of my door.

I shall ignore her   but she will persist.

Then   I shall call out
inform her I am counting
              Perhaps give a little yawn.

ANTHONY WILSON

Mustard

Whenever you fly over
we ask you to bring mustard,
'Dijon-only 90p - *incredible*.'

We eat it with sausage casserole,
once a week in the winter,
and you know it makes

a perfect vinaigrette, quite fiery.
You frown as I shake in
the Aromat.

Once, after presenting us the jar
you blurted 'It was the last thing
I thought would happen.

I wasn't looking for it
and definitely neither was she.'
At the end

a knife peers hopefully
into the jar as we angle it
to the light,

then tocks around
the mustard-streaked walls,
lonely and hollow.

MARY MAHER

Becoming Cupboard Conscious

She can be opened wide and wider
her shelves lined with tit-bits for
taste buds and dishfuls of love.
You'll need two arms and big eyes to scan
her take-me-down and come-again supplies. If
you have more than one tongue so much the better
to lick the foreign delicacies.
                                        You will tell her
by the company she keeps - nearby doorsteps
so huge your stomach will stumble, a kitchen
in which to loiter with no intention of picking up
crumbs, a place in fact for not holding back:
give her emptied bags your smell of approcal,
the ticks on her lists - cross them, kiss kiss kiss.
There will be her mother's mother's wooden spoons
and milk pans, rings so radiant fingers
will burn constantly. There will be salt
to season early stiffings, none needed to throw
for luck. There will be a whiff of apron-string
attachment, a back-door coat hooked up in haste.

JOHN HARVEY

Safeway

I like a woman who knows her way to Safeway
but will pack me off there anyway,
a list fixed to the refrigerator door -
"wonderful lettuce," "big dill," "great
tomatoes," "serious bread."
Who will be there when I get home,
closed inside her dark room, the
safety light glowing red, or cross-
legged on the floor, staring at the frets
of her guitar, putting the finishing
touches to a song. And I will tip-toe
around her, juggling packages and
misshapen bags, wallet, checked-off
list and keys. Place each and every
thing quietly in the place bestowed
for it - as quietly as lollo rosso
wrapped in cellophane will agree
to go. But a woman who also,
unexpectedly, will slide her hands
across my eyes the instant I step
through the door and have me turn
towards her face, the soft grey
vest across her breasts,
the sweet and supple sweetness of her skin.
And after we have risen from the wreck
of fallen groceries, either she or I
will slide a garlic-basted chicken

from its bag, uncork a bottle
of that Merlot and take them both
to bed, sitting in the soon-to-be
sweaty whiteness of sheets, breaking
the chicken with our hands and eating it,
aware of the joy of this and each other's
eyes, the juice that runs along our fingers
and gathers in the deft spaces inside
our arms and behind our knees, waiting
to be found there later, savoured, licked away.

Contributors

Chris Banks was brought up on herring and kippers in the Isle of Man. She still likes most smoked foods and adores anything spicy. She is on a quest for the ultimate kipper curry. When she is not eating, Chris is counselling, training counselling groups or writing poems. Her work has been published in many magazines and anthologies. *Watching the Home Movies* is available from Odyssey Press and contains **The Watermelon Sellers**.

David Bateman is a performance poet based in Liverpool His first full-length collection is *Curse Of The Killer Hedge* (Iron Press 1996). He teaches Creative Writing for the University of Liverpool and he counts his poker winnings in Mars Bars.

Catherine Benson was born in Yorkshire, brought up in the Highlands of Scotland. She is married, with grown-up children and grandchildren. Has been published in various anthologies and is currently working on a collection of poems called, 'Domestic Issues', so, often found dusting down dactyls, polishing pentameters, basting ballades or cooking up a kyrielle.

Judi Benson was formerly the editor of *Foolscap* and is co-editor with Ken Smith of *Klaonica: Poems for Bosnia* (Bloodaxe); Co-editor with Ogneta Falk of *The Long Pale Corridor*, Contemporary poems of bereavement (Bloodaxe). A selection of her poems *Somewhere Else* was published by Turret Books. *Cooking with Mae West* was a Turret Broadsheet

Patricia Bishop lives on the borders of everything. She has had work in many magazines and anthologies. Her books include *Aubergine is a Gravid Woman* (Headland) and *Double Exposure*. She recently won an Arts Council/BBC award for her part in an experimental poetry programme on BBC Radio 5.She hates garlic.

Gillie Bolton works with doctors and nurses who write stories and poems about their work, for professional development. They also offer their patients 'Writing Therapy'. Her past includes milk puddings in Epping Forest, bread and water in Cambridge, tea with evaporated milk in gypsy vans. Now she prefers champagne in bed on Christmas morning.

Sandra Booth - when she is not eating Vindaloos (preferably very hot) she works part time in a Family Planning Clinic and the rest of the time in the home attempting to satsfy the appetites of two teenage sons and a husband. Vindaloo is her second published poem.

Anne Born's tenth collection is due from Headland Publications this year. She believes picnics are the best way of eating, provided there's a supply of harmonic sun rather than stormy weather. Al fresco was ever the best table-setting for un repas à deux, even with wasps in the wine and a hornet's nest stirring in the trees.

Phil Bowen worked in pubs and clubs in Liverpool on a part-time basis before joining Grand Metropolitan in 1981, managing to stick it out until 1992. Is a big fan of the Dry Martini - 'one is necessary, two are dangerous, and three aren't enough'.

Peter Carpenter was born in Epsom, never sampled the local salts or water, but frequented 'The Amato' in the days of Doug and Brenda; converted long-standing vegetarian wife by torturing her with bacon; food references in his poetry include shallots, candy floss, stale crisps, moules, crab apples and oysters. He was a prizewinner in the 1995 Cardiff International Poetry Competition and has had many poems in magazines.

Tony Charles can almost remember fruit rationing; maybe that's why he loves the stuff. He divides his time between writing, performing, training, publishing **Headlock** and trying to teach an old dog new tricks. That fruit, though: it's best when all the juice runs down, isn't it?

Debjani Chatterjee was born in India and grew up in various Asian countries where she enjoyed lots of coconut milk. Her poetry books include *I Was That Woman* (Hippopotamus Press) and *The Sun Rises in the North* (Smith Doorstop Books). Her poems have won several international prizes. She has edited several books, including *Sweet and Sour* (Bengali Women's Support Group), a food anthology of prose, poetry and recipes.

Jane Clarkson was born and brought up in Exeter, and recently returned to live there after 17 years living as an adopted 'Northerner' in Lancashire. Leads 2 lives - one working in the Financial Services Industry, the other as a poet and performer. She is Co-organiser of Exe Lit - the Exeter Literary Festival (95 and 96) and member of the Devon River Poets. She believes that there is one major disadvantage to living in the South - no-one seems to know how to make good fish and chips.

Mandy Coe - based in Liverpool, Mandy Coe performs her work and teaches creative writing at venues across the North West. A performance poet of exceeding directness she is open about her eating 'I admit I do it ... at least four or five times a day.' In an interview with the Adam Smith Institute Periodical she argues '...it is the Nanny State attitude that is to blame. They think we can be forced out of this habit by low wages and benefits. I say sod 'em! I say don't let them stop us - hell, let's do it in public!'

Sarah Cowie is a Welsh American poet in Liverpool. She first performed her poetry at the age of eleven at a Gamanva Gani in Vermont. She re-established her performance poetry career in Cardiff in 1988. Sarah has a book coming out soon with Spike Press.

David Crystal's favourite food is Paella , to be eaten in Spain, outdoors on a big open fire.

Edmund Cusick was formerly a Lexicographer for the OED and Lecturer in English Literature at the University of Wales, Lampeter. He now teaches imaginative Writing at Liverpool John Moores University. He aquired a taste for marmalade and bacon sandwiches in a remote region of Scotland where tomato ketchup is unknown, and it has not left him. He lived for five years in a convent, where he learned the secret of the perfect chocolate sauce, involving cocoa, golden syrup, and butter.

John Daniel has been published by Faber and Faber (*Introduction 1*) and *Swallow* (23 Modern British Poets). He won Devon and Exeter Poetry Prize 1995. He hates monosodium glutomate and loves ice cream.

Alison Dunne was born hungry in the 60's and has been fond of eating ever since. Writing (and custard creams) kept her sane when she was at home with small children. She is Literature Development Officer for Leicestershire, Adult Ed. Tutor and half of Gas & Air - lardy poets who perform anywhere. Her work has been published, won prizes and been broadcast on Radio 4.

Yvonne M Fee was born in Southport. After a career in Nursing and bringing up a family she now has time to concentrate on her writing.

Duncan Forbes has had poems on radio (*Poetry Please*) and in Faber's *Poetry Introduction 5*. He studied English at Oxford and has since published three collections of poems: *August Autumn* (Secker), *Public & Confidential* and *Taking Liberties* (Enitharmon). His food and drink dislikes include fishbones, celery and parsnips. Likes are numerous and include good cooking, fine wines, variety, spice, lyrics and life.

Rebecca Goss is 23 years old and has just completed an MA in Creative Writing at Cardiff University. At sixteen she won the W H Smith Young Writers Competition and went on to do a BA in English at Liverpool John Moores University. Her first pamphlet *KEEPING HOUSTON TIME* is published by Slow Dancer Press.

John Harvey has been the publisher of *SLOW DANCER PRESS* since 1977. *STILL WATER*, the most recent of his Charlie Resnick crime novels - in which our hero makes and devours many a brave sandwich - is published by Heinemann.

Madeleine Heaney has worked as a Creative Writing Tutor for Leicester

University and is now Literature Development Officer for Northampton. Gone are the student days of waiting for buses in Edinburgh in driving wind and rain, eating chips and feeling guilty. Chips still induce guilt - but what delicious guilt!

Hilaire is a caffeine addict who is also partial to a drop of red wine. As a little girl she refused to eat anything except apricots. For the last twelve years she has been a vegetarian, and believes coriander is a form of human catnip. She lives with a non-gourmet, abstemious pop star.

Selima Hill lives in a small seaside town with her 3 children, 3 grandchildren 3 dogs, 29 ducks and 7 collections - the most recent, *Violet*, published by Bloodaxe. Her favourite food is chocolate-coated Bath Olivers. Her favourite drink is vanilla-flavoured Rice Dream rice milk.

Hazel Hills learnt to cook plainly from older women relatives and treasures the recipes written out by them for her - which raise the same memories & associations as an old family patchword quilt . Her poems and short stories have appeared in a variety of literary mags and anthologies in the UK and NZ.

Sidney Hoddes has been cooking and serving poems on Merseyside and beyond since the mid-sixties. He has had work in small magazines and his collections of poems include *Menu*, *Collage I* and *Poems About*.

Doris Hulme is a Yorkshire woman reared on roast beef when farming was organic. She still finds pasta feels like warmed-up slugs but, apart from this, enjoys almost anything that someone else has cooked, especially if it's accompanied by a good, dry red wine.

Hazel Jones lives near Crediton and is a tutor in Creative Writing at Exeter University. She prefers to make love on an empty stomach.

Kathleen Jones regards cooking as a kind of sorcery and practises it as often as possible. Four children and ten years in the Middle East and Africa have widened her repertoire considerably. She now lives in the Lake District and her books include *Learning not to be First: the Life of Christina Rossetti* OUP, *Unwritten Lives* Redbeck Press and *A Passionate Sisterhood: the wives, sisters and daughters of the Lake Poets* Constable.

Margaret Kirke spent a recent winter eating her way around the ex-communist European states from Prague to Estonia. She became very fond of dumplings and now knows that the best coffee and pastries can be found in Riga, Latvia. She didn't like Estonian red cabbage juice drink.

Helen Kitson lives in Manchester where she works part-time as a legal secretary. She has published a pamphlet (*Seeing's Believing*, Scratch) and a full-length collection (*Love Among the Guilty*, Bloodaxe). She describes herself as a hedonistic vegetarian with a heavy chocolate habit.

Linda Lamus is a journalist living in Bristol. She travels extensively and enjoys trying exotic food and drinks in far flung places. One of her most traumatic experiences when travelling was having Mars Bars stolen from her luggage at Tashkent airpot. *New Orleans* won first prize in the 95 Quartos Magazine Competition, first prize in the 95 Balwest Writers Competition and was a runner up in the Orillia International Poetry Festival 1996 Stephen Leacock Poetry Competition in Canada.

John Latham loves Jamaican Rum, cold spring water, Boursin, sharp English apples and detests almond paste and canned soft drinks. His poetry books include *From the Other Side of the Street* and *All-Clear* (Peterloo Poets). He has won many poetry competitions and has had stories and plays broadcast on Radio 4.

Mary Maher loves mugs, talking with friends in kitchens, hands round hot drinks, noses dipping into steam. Not surprising with collections called *Snowfruit* and *Cold Flushes* (both Stride).

Ruth L Malkin comes from the Midlands but now lives in Bradford; city of spices. This vibrant backdrop adds a certain piquancy to her writing. Her prose poem, Bruises, was inspired by a writing workshop led by Chenjare Hove.

William Oxley is a poet addicted to long poems (he co-edits the *Long Poem Group Newsletter*, and Salzburg Univeristy published his *Collected Longer Poems* in 1994) and to long meals. A 'main course man' really, his favourite starter is brie in bacon, and he thinks a good steak is as hard to beat as it is to cook just right. Always partial to the touch of garlic and a glass of red wine.

Margaret Padwick is a member of Brighton Poets and Chanctonbury Writers. She finds the role played by food in relationships endlessly fascinating. As she hates cooking her favourite foods are always those prepared by someone else.

William Park was born in '62, West London and was a Gregory Award winner in 1990. He has had poems in *The Observer*, *Poetry Review* etc. Now following Tibetan Buddhism, enjoys films like The Piano and The Spirit of the Beehive, and eats dried mango slices, but most of all chocolate, then some more, and still stays svelte and rangy.

Mario Petrucci - his favourite imbibings are a cool draught of West-of-Ireland cliff air, the wheeling curlews still in it; a sextuple helping of fried mushrooms and eggs, 11am, in a parallel universe where cholesterol simply isn't possible. Gustatory Nightmare: At the height of passion, discovering a two-day-old granule of pâté de foie gras between your partner's molars. His latest book is *Shrapnel and Sheets* published by Headland Press.

128

Joan Poulson is a prize-winning poet and freelance writer. She likes avocado with lemon juice and salt; fresh mango; rich dark chocolate mousse; newly baked crusty bread thickly spread with butter. She dislikes: boiled most things, especially vegetables.

Maurice Riordan was born in County Cork in 1953 and now lives in South London. He teaches part-time. His books include *A Word from the Loki* published by Faber.

Neil Rollinson eats Tagliatelle Putanesca with whole roasted garlic bulbs, crusty white rolls and cheap red wine.

Daphne Schiller has an M.A. in Creative Writing from the University of East Anglia, and has published poems, short stories and articles. She is a teacher and member of Ver Poets. She is fond of Italian food and aubergines.

Myra Schneider lives in North London and has had six collections of poetry published, the most recent is *Exits* (Enitharmon). She has had novels for children and teenagers published by Heinemann and is currently co-writing a book, *Writing for Self Discovery* with John Killick. She loves Indian food, pasta, fruit, vegetables, salad, baked potatoes, toast and marmalade, chocolate, eats a lot of vegetarian food and when in the mood much enjoys cooking.

Steve Sims says he is fat and past it, but likes to fantasise in Crediton, a better place to do it than Debiton.

Ken Smith has had several books of poetry published, most of them from Bloodaxe, the most recent being *Tender to the Queen of Spain*, and two non-fiction works: *Inside Time* (Harrap and Mandarin p/b) and *Berlin, coming in from the cold* (Hamish Hamilton and Penguin p/b). He has a marked and acknowledged liking for vodka, red wine and PG Tips. Food: fish, seafood, and any meat but mad cow; He has a sweet tooth for cakes, biscuits, ice cream (which he makes). His ideal meal is starter and sweet, cutting out the middle bit.

Mary Taylor - nine years as an NHS nutritionist drove her to write poetry. Worse, to give up her job and do an MA in Creative Writing. She emerged from that feast in 1994 and is now browning off 'Iona', her MA project, hopefully for publication. Favourite foods: Tropical! Salt fish served with roast plantain; fresh pineapple; Bounty choc-ices and Malibu punch.

Fran Shortridge has been writing poetry for about 3 years. She worked for five years in a family owned bakery and the best thing about this was consuming any reject biscuits while still warm. Her poems have been published in many magazines.

Nigel Slater's *Real Fast Food*, *Real Fast Puddings* (Penguin) and *The 30*

Minute Cook (Michael Joseph) are best-selling books. He writes for Sainsbury's magazine. He says he writes as he cooks; there is often sauce on the screen and crumbs in the keyboard.

Jane Spiro has published 2 books of stories for language learners, articles for literature teachers, and poems in journals and anthologies. She plays the violin, and tries to carry her violin wherever she goes. Her addictions are chocolate, pineapple and peanuts (not together), salads with avocado and pine-nuts, muesli with dates and yoghurt, and fresh tuna lightly grilled straight from the sea. All chicken concoctions are part of her primal memory, particularly chicken soup with noodles and dumplings.

Mandy Sutter lives in Leeds, where she works as a freelance trainer. Poetry collections are: *Permission to Stare* (Slow Dancer '94) and *Game* (Smith/Doorstop '95). She has published two educational plays, and short stories have appeared in various magazines. Her favourite foods - usually Turkish, appear regularly in her work, and she thinks you can tell a lot about a culture by the quality and price of its bread.

Gordon Wardman lives and writes in Essex and his latest collection is *Trolleytown* (Dog). He is, by preference, a fish eater. Favourite meal - oysters and champagne followed by smoked salmon and champagne. Cooks curry, chilli con carne etc because that's the sort of thing men learn to cook at university.

Gregory Warren Wilson is a violinist. He was a member of the Razumovsky String Quartet for three years, and the London Mozart Players for ten, touring internationally with them. Last year his first collection, *Preserving Lemons* won the Staple First Edition Award, and *Hanging Windchimes in a Vacuum* won the Tears in the Fence pamphlet competition. Having lived in Florence, he is gastronomically inseparable from la Pasta. Pièce de résistance - tortiglioni with asparagus, cream, olive oil and Parmesan. Followed by stewed cherries, Droste chocolate and peach Schnapps.

Anthony Wilson's first collection *How Far From Here is Home?* (Stride) was shortlisted for the Arts Council Award 1996. Big passions for cheese fondue, chicken rogan and Tesco's Chilean Cabernet Sauvignon. Big dislikes are: gooseberries, anchovies and white wine between October and May.

Sally Young worked in London as a journalist specialising in music and show-business before moving to the West Country where she continued a freelance career. Current work has appeared in a number for anthologies. She organises monthly literary lunches in Exeter and is a keen gardener.